AMESLAN

An Introduction to American Sign Language

by

Louie J. Fant, Jr.

DEDICATED TO
The beautiful people who hear
"the rustle of a star"

Cover Design by John Stukey

Dave Robinson

Standard Book Number 0-913072-03-6

Printed in the United States of America

Copyright © 1972 by Louie J. Fant, Jr.

Library of Congress Card No. 72-90793

Published by National Association of the Deaf
814 Thayer Avenue
Silver Spring, Maryland 20910

Reprinted 1973

FOREWORD

There is a great deal of misunderstanding with regard to sign language as it is used by deaf people. Therefore, I feel the necessity to attempt to clarify some of the mystery before encouraging the reader further in this book.

First of all, sign language does not consist of fingerspelling. The reader has probably had some contact with the manual alphabet, which is used to fingerspell words. Fingerspelling is nothing more than the presentation of spoken English in a visual-manual medium, just as writing is the presentation of spoken English in visual-printed form, the Morse Code is another aural system for presenting English. Neither fingerspelling, writing, nor Morse Code constitute a language, they are merely media for conveying a language. Fingerspelling is used by deaf people, but it alone does not constitute a language.

Secondly, there is no such thing as a single Sign Language. The terms, Sign Language, refer to any and all gesture languages. The American Indians use a sign language; hearing people, particulary the Latin, European, and Near Eastern ones, use a huge variety of gestures; deaf people in each country have their own sign language; and within the United States there are at least two distinguishable sign languages used. This book concerns itself with one sign language, Ameslan, which is one of the two sign languages used in the United States.

The two sign languages used most by American Deaf people are Siglish and Ameslan. Both these labels have only recently been coined in an effort to see more clearly what we are dealing with. That is to say, both languages have been extant since sign language was brought to this country from France by Thomas Gallaudet and Laurent Clerc in the early Nineteenth Century. Traditionally the two sign languages have been referred to in descriptive terms: Siglish was "signing in proper English order," "grammatical sign language," "schoolroom signing," "proper signing," "high verbal sign language," etc.; Ameslan was "real deaf sign language," "'deaf' deaf language," "street signing," "low verbal sign language," etc. One could not talk about sign language without constantly prefacing his remarks with some such description. So, in the last couple of years, the terms Siglish and Ameslan have come into being as an effort to make it simpler to designate what sign language one is talking about.

Siglish is an acronym made from the two words, signed English. Siglish is sign language that follows the English grammatical system. It is English presented visually on the hands, rather than orally by the voice.

Ameslan is an acronym made from the words, American sign language. Ameslan does not follow the English grammatical scheme. It is a wholly different language from English. In its structure, it has more in common with Chinese than English.

Confusion arises because both Siglish and Ameslan use identical signs. It is the manner in which the signs are put together that distinguishes Siglish from Ameslan. In other words, they share the same sign-vocabulary, but do not share the same sign-order. Siglish strings signs together (with the aid of fingerspelling) in the same order as English. Ameslan, on the other hand, strings those same signs together in its own unique way.

Siglish is an attempt to blend English and Ameslan together.

Ameslan and English being two distinct languages, and Siglish being a language derived from both Ameslan and English. From Ameslan it takes the signs, from English it takes the word order, and makes far more use of fingerspelling.

In order to understand why Siglish exists, the reader must have this brief introduction to the nature of the impact of deafness on language acquisition. Hearing children learn English from constantly hearing it over and over. They imitate what they hear. Adults correct the child when he errs in his spoken English. The child begins to hear his own mistakes and corrects them himself. He recognizes an error, not because he knows a rule of grammar that has been violated, but simply by the fact that it does not sound right. By the time the hearing child is seven or eight, he speaks grammatically correct English, provided of course, he has had adult models who spoke correct English. From seven years of age on, he merely refines the basic patterns he learned during those first few years.

Obviously, a deaf child cannot learn English this way. In order for him to learn English, it must be presented to him visually. Siglish was developed in an effort to teach English to deaf children. Fingerspelling and lipreading are incorporated into Siglish to enhance further the visualization of spoken English.

Deaf children, when allowed to do so, develop their own sign language which they use among themselves. That is, in class they will attempt to use Siglish, and on the play-ground they will use their own sign language. The sign language they invent for them-selves resembles Ameslan in its grammatical structure, though it will differ in many of its signs.

As the children grow older, and come into contact with older deaf children and adults, their invented sign language comes more and more to resemble Ameslan. The process is quickened by deaf children of deaf parents who use Ameslan in the home. Naturally, these deaf children pass on to the other deaf children the more standardized signs of Ameslan.

Thus, each school for deaf children where signing is permitted, produces signs which are carried on into adulthood, and are not known beyond the influence of their school. This situation is somewhat analogous to dialects in spoken languages. They are commonly referred to as "local" signs. There are not so many of them, however, that a deaf person from one part of the country cannot understand a person from another part. Often the differences between a local sign and a standard sign are so slight that the uninitiated may see no difference at all. On the other hand, a hearing person learning Ameslan, may see no similarity between a local and a standard sign which would be easily seen by a deaf person.

Another factor which encourages these "dialect" signs is that most schools for deaf children do not teach Ameslan to the young deaf child. This is done on the supposition that if the deaf child uses Ameslan, it will impede his progress in learning English. This is a highly debatable issue which I do not want to go in to at this time. These same schools, however, will use Siglish when the child is around twelve years of age. If the deaf child had not learned Ameslan on his own, he could not use Siglish. So, in effect, the school recognizes the need for the deaf child to develop some kind of sign language, but does little or nothing to encourage him in this endeavor.

A further word must be said as to the acquisition of English by deaf people. It is generally agreed that most deaf adults handle English on about a fifth or sixth grade level, whereas most hearing adults are around the ninth or tenth grade level. The reasons for this huge difference are several, but basically it boils down to the fact that for the typical deaf person, English is a second language, a foreign language. Just as most hearing people who study a foreign language, rarely master it, a deaf person rarely masters English. Whatever the factors are that work against hearing people in learning second languages, those same factors work against deaf people.

Another factor that has arrested the deaf person's effort to learn English is that he is required to use English in order to learn English. A Spanish, or French, or German speaking child has the advantage of being taught English through the use of his own native language. When his mastery of English reaches a certain proficiency level, then he is required to use only English, thus his progress is accelerated. A total immersion into a second language from the very beginning is extremely difficult for most people to handle. The average hearing person will not survive. It becomes too frustrating not to understand, not to be able to ask a simple question, not to be able to relax and chat in his native tongue. Nevertheless, this is what is generally expected of deaf children.

Now, because the typical deaf person functions on the fifth or sixth grade level, in terms of his ability to read and write English, he does not understand Siglish as well as he understands Ameslan. Siglish is, remember, only manually signed English. If a deaf person does not read or write English fluently, he will understand English only slightly better when it is presented manually. Therefore, if the reader wishes to learn to communicate fluently with the typical deaf adult or child, he must learn Ameslan. Ameslan is the deaf person's language. To be sure, a typical deaf person will get the gist of what you sign in Siglish, but in Ameslan he gets all of it, not merely the gist.

When a hearing person has mastered Ameslan, it is not difficult at all to sign in Siglish. He uses the same signs, and merely arranges them in English order. When he converses with a deaf person who prefers Siglish, he will have no problem following along. If the deaf person prefers Ameslan, then the hearing person can slip into that groove. In short, once having mastered Ameslan, the hearing person may go either route. If, however, he has learned only Siglish, he can only go one way, and thus is limited to one-way streets.

I would close this section with this bit of admonition. Do not judge deaf people by their English. Their halting English in no way reflects on their intelligence or ambition. They are as bright, witty, cheerful, and ambitious as hearing people (often more so). They have tried, often under incredibly harsh conditions, to master English. They have done their best, and if they fall short, it is through no fault of their own. Before you judge, ask yourself how well you would fare if you were required to learn a foreign language under comparable conditions. Suppose, for example, you were in a sound proof, glass booth, equipped only with a pad and pencil. Outside the booth is your instructor who speaks, reads, and writes only Japanese. How long would it take you to learn Japanese? How well would you learn it?

HOW TO USE THIS BOOK

This book is not a dictionary of signs. There are around 375 signs covered in these lessons, and that comprises a small portion of the several thousand signs of Ameslan. The objective of this book is not to teach signs, but rather how to put signs together the way deaf people do. That is, after all, what is involved in learning a language. This book is not concerned with vocabulary development, but with the structure of the language. Vocabulary growth comes with communication with deaf people.

Secondly, this book is not a self-teaching device. It is impossible to capture in a still photograph or drawing the movement which is essential to a sign. You must have a fluent signer demonstrate the signs for you. The photographs merely help you recall what you were shown.

In the explanatory material, underlined words are signs. For example: next week are two signs, whereas next week is one sign. Words in quotation marks are English words, not signs. For example; "Do you?" is signed ask question.

An asterisk directs your attention to notes at the end of the lessons.

There is available a set of films made especially to accompany this book. For each lesson, there is a corresponding film which provides practice in reading Ameslan.

After a lesson has been covered thoroughly in class, the students should view the film for that lesson, on his own. He should view the films as many times as necessary, until he can read each sentence on the film. The sentences are the same ones in the lesson.

Although the book may be used without the films, progress in learning to read signs is greatly accelerated when the films are incorporated.

The 14 films are color, and approximately 5 minutes in length. They are housed in Super 8 cartridges and can be run on the Kodak Ektagraphic 120 projector. They may be purchased from the National Association of the Deaf, 814 Thayer Avenue, Silver Spring, Maryland, 20910, or from Joyce Motion Picture Company, 8320 Reseda Boulevard, Northridge, California, 91324.

Whenever you see the picture of the sign for "movie"

at the end of the lesson, that is when the film should be viewed.

TABLE OF CONTENTS

1. Good morning. Good afternoon. Good night.

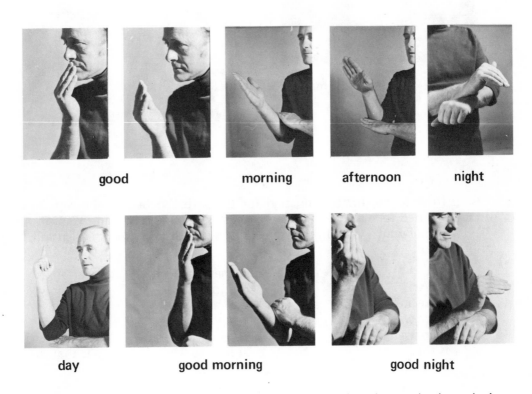

good   morning   afternoon   night

day   good morning   good night

The expression, "Good night," is used both as a salutation and when closing a conversation.

2. Hello! I'm glad to see you.

hello   glad, happy

see

you

I   I, me

true

A.   In Ameslan, there is no sign for the verb "to be." if the sign, true is sub-
     stituted for "am" in this sentence, the meaning is altered to, "I am truly glad
     to see you!" Listed below are other ways to translate this sign into English:

it is	is the truth	certain
it was	am truly	certainly
there are	am really	indeed
there was	real	actual
there were	sure	actually
is true	surely	Is that so?

B.   The sight line in Ameslan is very important. This is an imaginary line between
     signer and observer, i.e., "speaker" and "listener." Whenever a sign such as see
     moves along the sight line towards the observer, the pronouns "I" and "you"
     are implied, thus they need not be signed. That is to say, instead of signing I
     see you, you need to sign only see. Since the sign moves from "I" towards
     "you," the pronouns are built into the movement. Later you will learn other
     uses for the sight line.

C.   There is no infinitive form for verb signs, since the signs are not inflected as
     are verbs in some spoken languages. In English, we say,"to see, I see, you see,
     he sees, she saw, we have seen, etc." but in Ameslan the sign see remains the
     same throughout, and the "to" is not signed.

D.   Many signs such as happy must be repeated.

2

3. How are you?

how

A. Remember, the "are" is not signed, but is understood, unless you wish to emphasize the statement.

B. Although there is a sign in Ameslan which indicates that you are asking a question, it is used only to emphasize that fact. In ordinary questions, your facial expression, the tilt of your head, a slight hunch of the shoulders make it clear you are asking a question. These physical cues are analagous to the rise and fall of your voice when you ask a question in a spoken language.

4. How do you feel?

feel

A. Ameslan has no sign for "do" when it is used in this manner.

B. It is obvious that the signer is asking the observer how he feels, so it is not necessary to sign you.

5.   I'm fine, thank you. I'm tired. I'm sick. I'm lousy. I'm terrible.

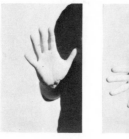

fine, excellent, superb   tired, worn out, fatigued, weary

sick, ill   lousy

awful, terrible   thank you

A.   Again, it is not necessary to sign "I'm".

B.   In general, the pronouns "I" and "you" are signed only for emphasis.

6. I'm glad you feel better.

_____er   **better**

A. In order to form comparatives and superlatives, such as "good," "better," "best," add the er sign to the adjective. Literally, "better" is "gooder," (good + er); "best" is good+er, except that the er sign rises higher, giving it more emphasis.

B. Practice forming these:

Comparatives	Superlatives
finer	finest
tireder	tiredest
sicker	sickest
lousier	lousiest
awfuler	awfulest

7. I'm happy to meet you.

meet

The sign meet moves along the sight line when you are introduced to a person, thus it implies "you."

8. We met once, don't you remember?

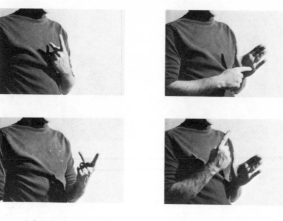

we (two persons)   **once**

not   **remember, recall**

A. There are numerous ways of negating statements in Ameslan. The sign not is one of the most common. However, by far the most common way is simply to shake the head. In the sentence, "Don't you remember?" sign remember while you shake your head. There is no need to sign not, and of course, you is not signed.

B. There is no past or future tense in Ameslan. Instead of changing the sign to indicate tense, as we do in English (meet-met, see-saw, do-did, etc.), Ameslan uses other signs. In the sentence, "We met once, don't you remember?" the sign once refers to the past, thus clearly establishing the time. Signs such as once are called time-indicators.

9. Yes, I remember.

yes

6

10. No, I don't remember.

no

Again, as in Number 8, this sentence may be reduced to simply signing remember while shaking the head "no." Ameslan tends to condense whenever possible.

11. I'm sorry, forgive me.

sorry, regret   **pardon, excuse, forgive**

Do not sign <u>me</u> in, "forgive me."

12. That's all right, I understand.

all right   **understand, comprehend**

Normally the sign <u>all right</u> is made with just one movement. In this sentence, two small, quick movements are used to emphasize that it is a casual, unimportant circumstance.

13. Please, don't feel sorry.

don't   **please, be pleased, enjoy**

The sign <u>don't</u> is used primarily to give a negative command.

14. I have to go now.

must, have to, got to, need to, necessary, ought, should, supposed to

go   **now**

The sign <u>must</u> is used to convey all of the following:

must	need to	ought to	have to
	need	should	have got to
	necessary	supposed to	had to

8

15. Goodbye, see you later.

goodbye

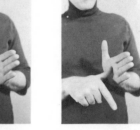

later, afterwhile, awhile

16.   What are you doing?

what   **perform, do**

The sign <u>perform</u> is used only to mean an action, a performance, an activity, etc. Never use it for the English "do" in, "Do you feel well?"

17.   I'm taking a class in signing.

take up   **class, group**   **in**

sign

A.   Ameslan has no articles (a, an, the).

B.   The sign <u>take up</u> means specifically "to take up an activity." Never use it in such sentences as, "Take the book home," "He took ill," "Have you taken your medicine," or "Take my advice."

18.   I'm learning to sign.

learn

The sign <u>learn</u> is ordinarily made with only one movement. If, however, you wished to indicate that the "learning" you are going through is hard work, or takes a great deal of time, you would repeat the movement twice.

19.   I'm learning sign language.

language

sentence

Ameslan, like other languages, is constantly changing. The sign <u>language</u> is an example of a sign in transition. Many people prefer the newer sign for "language," with 'L's" (first picture), using the older sign (second picture) for "sentence." Others, however, use the older sign for both "language" and "sentence". The newer sign is an example of what is called an initialized sign, that is, a sign that takes the first letter of the English word and adds it to the root sign.

20. I'm learning how to sign.

21. Why are you learning sign language?

why

22. Because I want to talk to deaf people.

because   **want**

converse, talk to   **with, together**   **people**

deaf

A. There are several signs in Ameslan for <u>talking</u> and <u>speaking</u>. The sign used here implies talking to a specific individual.

B. There are two signs for "deaf." The one in the first picture is the older, but both are acceptable.

23. It isn't easy to learn a new language.

easy, simple   new

    A.   The words, "It isn't" are translated by the sign <u>not</u>.

    B.   The sign <u>easy</u> has two repetitions of the movement.

24. You must study hard.

study   hard, difficult

25. There are many signs.

many

The idea "there are" is translated by the sign <u>true</u>. Refer to the list of expressions in 2, A. for the ways in which the <u>true</u> sign may be translated.

26. Deaf people converse by signing.

Ameslan drops many of the prepositions and conjunctions used in English. In this sentence, the sign <u>with</u> substitutes for the word "by." The sign <u>converse</u> is almost always accompanied by the sign <u>with</u>.

27. In this book, sign language is called Ameslan.

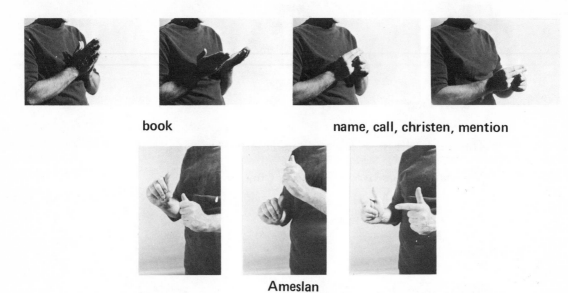

book   name, call, christen, mention

Ameslan

A. It is not considered impolite to point in Ameslan. Indeed, because pointing is used extensively, there are few pronoun signs. Whenever an object or person is visible, pointing is the most convenient way to refer to it.

B. The sign <u>name</u> belongs to a very small class of signs which have a noun form and a verb form. The verb form is shown here, and the noun form is shown in 53.

C. The word, Ameslan, is a newly coined word, thus the sign is also new. Therefore, use it only among your classmates, unless you are prepared to explain it.

28.   Have you eaten?

finish, complete   **eat, food**

The sign <u>finish</u> is often used as a time-indicator (see 8, B.) Listed below are the numerous ways in which this sign is translated:

A.   Examples of the time-indicator function of finish when it is used with a verb sign. In all of these, you sign only <u>finish</u> <u>eat</u>.

ate	did already finish eating
have eaten	did finish eating
had eaten	did eat
have already eaten	ate already
had already eaten	Have you eaten?
did already eat	Did you eat?
have already finished eating	Have you already eaten?
had already finished eating	Did you eat already?

B.   Meaning of the sign <u>finish</u> when it appears alone.

That's all. It's over. It's done. That's enough. It's finished.

29.   Not yet, have you?

not yet, late, tardy

A. The sign <u>not yet</u> is another often used time-indicator (see 8, B.) Listed below are the numerous ways in which this sign is translated:

  (1) Examples of the time-indicator function of the sign <u>not yet</u> when it appears with a verb sign. All of these are signed <u>not yet eat</u>.

haven't eaten yet   Haven't you eaten yet?
didn't eat yet   Didn't you eat yet?
hadn't eaten yet

  (2) Meaning of the sign <u>not yet</u> when it appears alone.

It's late.   It's too late.   Not yet.

B. The <u>not yet</u> sign is the only negative time-indicator sign. It not only refers to the past, but also states that a particular event did not occur. There is often an extremely subtle implication that the event might still occur, which is why the "yet" idea is included here. You may also use the <u>not</u> sign instead of the <u>not yet</u> sign in the examples in A1, above, but the "yet" idea is not implied. Generally, the sign <u>not</u> is used simply to deny that a fact is, or that an event occured.

C. In the sentence, "Not yet, have you?" it is not necessary to sign <u>finish</u> for "have you?" Just point with an inquisitive expression on your face.

30. I ate awhile ago.

awhile ago

The sign <u>awhile ago</u> is a time-indicator sign, so you need not use the sign <u>finish</u>.

16

31. I'm hungry, but I've got to practice my sentences.

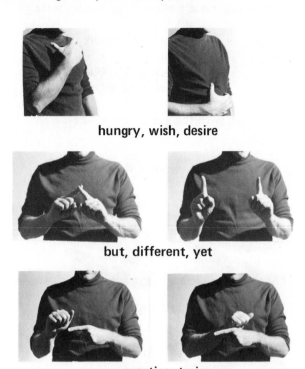

hungry, wish, desire

but, different, yet

practice, train

Sometimes when a sign is repeated, it indicates plurality. In the above sentence, the sign <u>sentence</u> is repeated for this purpose.

32. You still working on them?

still, yet

work   on

The sign <u>work</u>, like <u>learn,</u> is a sign which varies in meaning with the variation in the

17

speed, the size, and number of repetitions. Practice making the sign <u>work</u> indicating the following (facial expressions are also extremely important):

> work long hours
> work fast
> work that is boring
> work that is fascinating

Try the same four attitudes with the signs <u>learn</u> and <u>study</u>.

33.   I don't understand the meaning of some of the signs.

mean, intend, intention, purpose

some

A.   While you sign, "I don't understand," be sure to shake your head. Many people will even drop the "don't" and simply shake their heads when they sign <u>understand</u>, which naturally negates the sign and means "not understand."

B.   Ameslan has no sign for "of," so it is usually omitted. Sometimes other prepositions signs are substituted.

34.   Try to use them often.

try, attempt   **use**

often

A.   Often, the sign try is seen as an initialized sign, using "t's" for "try," "a's" for "attempt," and "s's" for "strive."

B.   Since there is no sign for "them," repeat the antecedent, which is, sign, so the sentence becomes, try use sign often.

35.   I do, but I'm still confused.

confuse, mix

For "I do", sign finish, since it implies that you "have already done that."

36.   Maybe you're not practicing enough.

maybe, perhaps

enough, plenty

37. That's not so!

that

A. The sign <u>that</u> also means <u>this</u>, <u>these</u>, <u>them</u>, <u>those</u>, <u>they</u>, <u>it</u>, and <u>the</u>. In general, the sign is used to refer to persons, places, and things that are not present, nor have they been established off the sight line. It is used most often in such expressions such as "That's not so!" "That's it!" "Oh, I see!" "That's what you mean!", etc.

B. There is no sign for "so." When "so" means "true," as it does here, use the sign <u>true</u>.

38. Let me see you again.

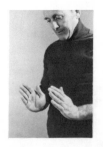

let, allow, permit

again

39.	I don't understand most of the signs.

most

A.	Remember that generally the "I don't" in sentences like this, is omitted. Shake the head while signing <u>understand</u>.

B.	The sign <u>most</u> is the root sign from which the <u>er</u> sign (see 6, A.) is taken.

40.	That's the trouble, you must understand the meanings.

trouble, worry

A.	Here is another example of when the sign <u>that</u> is used. Since there is no concrete person, place, or thing to which it refers, but rather an idea, the sign is used.

B.	The sign <u>mean</u> should be repeated two or three times to indicate plurality, just as <u>sentence</u> was repeated for plurality in 31.

41. I still confuse <u>not yet</u> and <u>not</u>.

and

Whenever you compare or contrast two things, place them on opposite sides of the sight line. In this sentence, it is also necessary to add the sign <u>sign</u> before both <u>not yet</u> and <u>not</u>. By doing this, you clarify what you are comparing. The sentence should be signed, <u>still</u> <u>confuse</u> <u>sign</u> <u>not yet</u> and <u>sign</u> <u>not</u>.

42.   Where's my typewriter?

where

my

typewriter, typing

43.   Where's my newspaper?

print

paper

A.   The sign print refers only to the printer's trade. It does not refer to print as in, "Print your name."

B.   The sign paper has two movements, but when it is combined with print, in newspaper, it has only one movement.

44.   I gave it to your friend.

give

your

friend

A.   The sign <u>give</u> must move at an angle away from the sight line, not along the sight line towards the observer. Whenever a third person, place, or thing is referred to, it must be placed to the side of the sight line. Practice this with, "I met your friend," and "I saw your friend."

B.   Ameslan relies heavily on context to clarify pronouns such as "it" in this sentence. Both the signer and observer know they are talking about the newspaper, so there is no need to sign it.

45.   I hadn't read it yet.

read

Remember, that "hadn't yet" is a negation of a past event so use <u>not yet.</u>

46. I'm sorry, I thought you had.

think

A. The sign <u>think</u> moves in a small circle on the brow, except when you wish to express the idea of a single thought. That is, the small circular movement implies "thinking," and the stationary finger with a nod of the head implies "think," or "a thought."

B. Remember that "you had" is signed as <u>finish.</u> If you forgot this, review the examples in 28.

47. Why didn't you ask me?

ask, request

48. You were gone to the movies.

go away

movies

There are several signs which indicate the idea, "go." The first sign was in 14. It is difficult to state any general principle as to which <u>go</u> sign one should use in a given situation. You develop a feeling for it as you gain experience. The sign given here is called the <u>go away</u> sign. It emphasizes the absence of someone rather than the going of someone. In other words, it stresses the fact that someone is not here, but somewhere else. Often the English verb "to leave" is translated by the <u>go away</u> sign.

49. I have to type up a list of things to memorize.

list, page of

thing

for

memorize

A. There is no sign for "up" when it is used as it is here. Other expressions such as "use up," "think up," "burn up," etc. are treated similarly.

B. The sign used here for "list" is more of a mime. It can also mean "a written passage," "a page full of something," etc.

C. Ordinarily, there is no attempt to translate the "to" in "to memorize," but you could use the sign <u>for.</u> The meaning would be "for memorizing."

50. I forgot to tell you something.

forget

only, always, someone, something, alone

tell

The sign <u>only</u> is elusive in meaning. In addition to "only," it also may mean "someone," and "always." To further perplex you, it also means "something." However, "always" is sometimes signed in a much larger circle, and sometimes the hand is lowered, pointing out instead of up. "Someone" is sometimes signed <u>only</u> <u>person</u>. "Something" is sometimes signed <u>only</u> <u>thing</u>. Practice signing these ideas both ways so you will be familiar with them.

51. Is it something about my typewriter?

about

52. Last night, I loaned it to your friend.

past, ago, last

lend, borrow

A. The sign past is another time-indicator sign. It refers to an event that happened as recent as last night, or a hundred years ago. When it is combined with the signs night, week, month, and year it means "last." Last week, and last year, however, have their own signs, which we shall come to later.

B. The sign lend also means "borrow," Ameslan recognizes no difference. The sentences, "Will you lend me a dime?" and "May I borrow a dime?" are identical in Ameslan.

C. Be sure you sign lend at an angle from the sight line towards "your friend."

A.   Hi! What are you doing?
I'm practicing my signs.
Are you learning sign language?
Yes, but there are so many signs.
Is sign language hard?
No, but I forget many signs.
Why do you want to learn sign language?
I want to learn how to talk to deaf people.
Do you enjoy learning sign language?
Yes, but it's not called sign language, it's called Ameslan.

B.   Hello! I'm glad to see you. Do you remember me?
Have I met you?
Yes, don't you remember?
No, I'm sorry, I don't.
Oh, that's all right, you and I took a class in Ameslan together.
Oh, yes, now I remember. Are you still taking the class?
Yes, why aren't you in the class?
I had to work, indeed, I must go to work now.
See you later.
Fine, goodbye.

C.   Hi!
Don't talk to me!
Why? What did I do?
You forgot to eat with me.
I forgot I was supposed to.
I wanted you to eat with me.
I'm sorry, I didn't understand.
Did you eat?
Not yet, you want to eat with me now?
No, I want to go to a movie.
All right, but I've gotta eat.

D.   Have you finished with the typewriter?
No, but I'm not using it now.
Fine, I'll use it and you read the book.
I've read that book.
Have you read the newspaper?
I've read most of it.
Why not try to memorize something?
I'm lousy at memorizing. What should I do?
Why ask me?
I should study the list of signs.
I'll talk to you later about that.
What do you mean?
Work on those signs.
I'm confused.

29

53. Almost all deaf people have name signs.

almost

all

possess, have   name

A. The sign <u>almost</u> has one movement, whereas the sign <u>easy</u> (see 23) has two, otherwise they are identical.

B. Here, the noun form of "name" is used. The sign is made with two movements. Review 27 B for the verb form.

54. What is your name sign?

55. I don't have one.

A. In English, "one" gets far more use than it does in Ameslan. Ordinarily, sign the idea or thing for which the word "one" stands, which in this sentence is the sign <u>sign</u>.

B. The more common way to sign this sentence is just: <u>have</u> <u>none</u>, dropping everything else. The <u>none</u> sign is the most common sign of negation. It means "none," "not any," "no one," and "nothing."

56. You must invent one.

invent, create

57. My name sign is _____.

Usually one takes the first letter of one's name and places it somewhere on the face, head, shoulders, arms, or upper torso. If one has a distinctive physical characteristic, such as a dimple, or moustache, the letter might be associated in some way with that characteristic. The name sign refers to the person, not to the name.

58. Let's sign a poem called Solomon Grundy.

poem, poetry

quotation marks

Solomon Grundy

born

marry   become

decline in health

die

bury, grave

story

32

Monday

Tuesday

Wednesday

Thursday

Friday

Saturday

Sunday

A. The sign quotation marks is used after the sign name ("called") here to make it clearer that you are giving the title to something.

B. The sign for Solomon Grundy is, of course, one invented by the author. Any other creation would serve just as well.

> Solomon Grundy,
> Born on Monday,
> Christened on Tuesday,
> Married on Wednesday,
> Took ill on Thursday, (C)
> Worse on Friday, (D)
> Died on Saturday,
> Buried on Sunday,
> This is the end, (E)
> of Solomon Grundy. (F)

C. The sign <u>become</u> is used in the expression "took ill," since this is the idea.

D. The sign <u>decline in health</u> is used only when a person is sinking towards death, or to imply that his mind is going as in senility.

E. "This is the end" is much clearer when signed <u>finish</u> <u>story</u>.

F. Since the previous line was signed <u>finish</u> <u>story</u>, we sign this line as <u>about</u> <u>Solomon</u> <u>Grundy</u>.

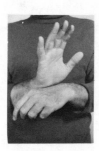

59. Do you like to watch television?

like, interesting, be interested in

watch, look at

television

The sign <u>like</u> is far more common than the <u>please</u> sign (see 13), when you wish to express the idea of "liking." The <u>like</u> sign appears with two hands and one hand. Generally, two hands emphasize that you like something very much. The <u>like</u> sign also means "interesting," although in certain parts of the country there is a slight variation in the way it is signed. Ameslan makes little distinction between liking something and finding something interesting.

60. I like some shows.

play, drama, show, act

61.   I don't like shows with a lot of talking.

much, a lot of

talk

A.   In English, "a lot of" may mean "much" as in "a lot of talking," or it may mean "many" as in "a lot of people." Since Ameslan has a sign for each of these (see 25 for many), you must decide which is meant before translating "a lot of" into Ameslan.

B.   Ameslan has several ways of signing "talk." This may seem curious at first, since deaf people do not speak very well, but they are great conversationalists. Therefore, they have a number of signs dealing with conversation. The first one you learned was converse (see 22). Now, the sign talk does not imply a conversation. In general, it refers to a kind of talking which is not directed to a specific person. It definitely is not the kind of talk one enjoys, for it has a slightly unsavory connotation of someone who talks too much. There are numerous ways to vary the movement of both hands, and the wriggling of the fingers to indicate numerous types of talking. Practice these examples:

  talk, and talk, and talk (one hand first, then two)
  talk rapidly
  talk slowly
  whispers
  talk mean, chew someone out

C.   The preposition "with" is not signed here. The sign with has a strong physical sense about it. You would use it in such sentences as "I saw you with him," "I'll go with you," and "I like coffee with cream," but not likely in "He talks with a lisp," "I write with my left hand," and "She sang with ardor." In other words, use the sign with when there is a sense of physical togetherness.

D.   Sentence 61 may be signed: (1) not like show much talk, or (2) not like show talk (using a variation which indicates "a lot of talking").

62.   I like shows with a lot of action.

action

The sign <u>action</u> is an enlargement of the sign <u>perform.</u>

63.   Talk shows are boring.

boring, dull, dry

A.   You need not sign <u>shows</u> here, since the context has already clearly estab-
       lished that you are talking about TV shows.

B.   The <u>talk</u> sign should indicate a great deal of talking.

64.   What kind of shows do you like best?

A.   The English "kind of" cannot be translated into Ameslan, sign; <u>what</u> <u>show.</u>

B.   Review 6,A. for an explanation for the sign <u>best.</u>

65.   I like football, basketball, baseball, swimming, track, wrestling, etc.

football   **basketball**

baseball

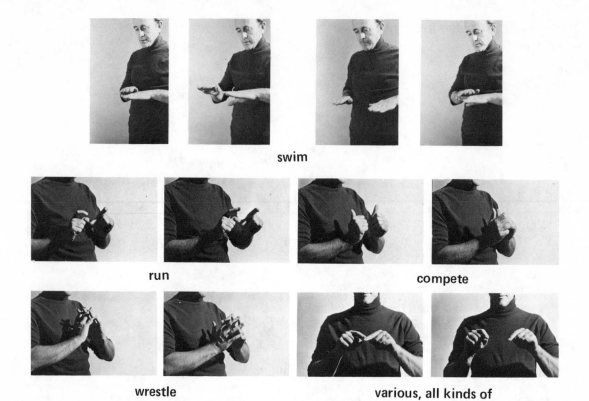

swim

run

compete

wrestle

various, all kinds of

There is no sign for "track," so we combine the two ideas of "run" and "compete." The sign <u>compete</u> also means "contest," "to run against," and "race."

66. What else do you like?

else, other, another

67. I like cowboy, war, and adventure movies.

cow

boy

war   hunt

travel

A.   There is no sign for "adventure," so you may sign whatever things "adventure" means to you. Here the author has chosen "hunting" and "traveling."

B.   The sign <u>boy</u> has two quick movements of the thumb touching the fingertips. The hand maintains contact with the forehead. The sign is altered slightly by moving it outward from the forehead to mean <u>male</u>, <u>man</u>, or <u>men</u>. This sign may also mean "mankind," and "human."

68.   I like comedies.

funny

69.   The old silent movies were the best.

silent, quiet   old

long time ago

A.   Deaf people do not refer to silent movies as "silent," since all movies are silent to them. They call them "sub-titled," or "captioned" movies, which they sign as <u>sentence</u> <u>movie.</u>

B.   The sign <u>long time ago,</u> is a time-indicator sign. It is used in this sentence to set the time when these type movies were popular. Therefore, the sentence ought to be signed, <u>long time ago</u> <u>sentence</u> <u>movie</u> <u>best.</u> You may use the sign <u>old</u> instead of <u>long time ago,</u> but the latter would be more common. It is clearer, because it establishes a time sense, whereas the sign <u>old</u> is only an adjective.

70.   When I watch a silent movie, I read the subtitles and understand everything clearly.

when

each, every   **clear**

As you sign this sentence, you should place <u>sentence</u> <u>movie</u> up where the screen of the theatre would be, as if you were actually sitting there watching the movie. Then, the sign <u>read</u> should show your eyes focused on and moving across the screen, not focused on a book in front of you as it is shown in 45.

71. There's so much talking in movies now days that I don't understand anything.

The sign now preceeds day to make "today," and night to make "tonight." The sign now day also means "now days". Frequently, when the context makes it clear, people will drop the sign day, and sign only now, meaning "today." This is rarely done with night, however. In other words, the sign now alone can mean "today," but it would seldom mean "tonight." Also when the sign now is combined with morning or afternoon, it is translated as "this morning," and "this afternoon."

* 72. I get captioned films from the government.

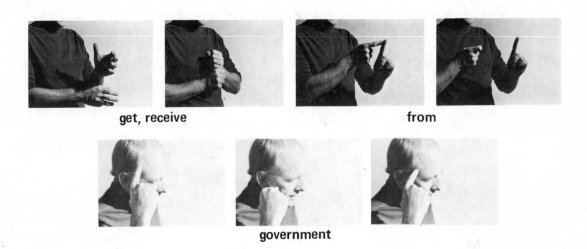

get, receive   from

government

The sign get means only "to receive." Never use it to translate such English expressions as "get up," "get going," "get out," etc.

73. I receive a film each month.

month

Sometimes the repetition of a sign indicates regularity. Here the sign month is repeated three or four times and moved to the side, indicating "every month," or "monthly". There is no need, of course, to sign each.

74. I go to my friend's home to see the movies.

go to

home

A. This sign for "go" is called the go to sign, because it implies going to a specific place. The other two signs you have learned so far are: (1) go (see 14), which is a general kind of sign, stressing "leaving," and (2) go away (see 48) which stresses "absence from here" rather than "going." The sign go to is perhaps most used of all the "going" signs.

B. The sign go to must move away from the sight line at an angle in this sentence, i.e., towards the friend's home.

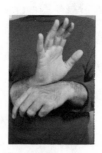

*75.   Every Saturday night, I go to the club.

every Saturday

club

A.   By moving a weekday sign downward, you indicate that something occurs weekly on that particular day.

B.   By repeating the go to sign, you get regularity again as you did with month (see 73.).

C.   There is no sign for "club," so you must fingerspell it.

76.   What do you do at the club?

A.   The first "do" in this sentence is not signed. The second "do" is signed perform.

B.   For the phrase "at the club," first simply point to the area indicated as to where the club is, then fingerspell "club."

77.   Meet other deaf people, play cards, dominoes, talk, etc.

play   card playing

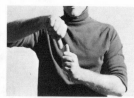

| dominoes | chat | associate, interact, fellowship, each other |

A.   The sign <u>meet</u> is given a twist, and moved around in a circle to indicate "meeting many people." This movement is done whenever you wish to expand a sign from referring to one person or thing, to referring to several or many persons or things.

B.   The sign <u>associate</u> is put in here, though it is not necessarily translated into English. It emphasizes the "meeting of people," and the warm interaction that usually takes place.

C.   The sign <u>chat</u> is the third sign for "talk." It indicates a warm, friendly, intimate kind of conversation.

78.   I don't want to go to the club. I don't know anybody there.

don't want

know, knowledge

don't know

A.   Several signs have negation built into them so that it is unnecessary to add any additional negative signs. The signs <u>don't know</u> and <u>don't want</u> are two such signs.

B.   For the "anybody" in this sentence, substitute the sign <u>people.</u>

C.   To indicate "there," just point to where the club is.

79. That doesn't matter, you'll make a lot of new friends.

nevertheless, doesn't matter, regardless, anyhow, irrespective

A. Ameslan does not "make" friends, but rather "meets" friends.

B. Watch the "a lot of," is it <u>much</u> or <u>many</u>?

80. You can, but I can't.

can   **can't**

A. Be sure to nod your head "yes," while signing <u>you can</u>, and shake it "no," while signing <u>I can't</u>.

B. Many people will reduce this sentence to merely pointing to "you" while shaking the head "yes," and point to "I" while shaking it "no."

81. Don't be silly.

stop   **silly, foolish, ridiculous, absurd**

Since Ameslan has no sign for "be," the command, "Don't be silly," cannot be signed. Instead, sign: <u>stop silly</u>.

82. Okay. May I go with you next Saturday?

Okay

next

A. Ameslan makes no distinction between "may" and "can", so it is always signed <u>can.</u>

B. The sign <u>with</u> is moved towards the area where the club has been placed. This movement implies "go with you," so "go" and "you" are not signed.

83. I can't go next Saturday, I'm going to my church for a banquet.

banquet   **church**

A. To indicate a banquet, or big meal, make the sign <u>eat</u> with both hands alternately, and repeat it twice. If it's a huge feast, you might add a mime showing the food piled up in a heap.

B. Be sure to place the church in a spot clearly different from where the club is. The best place is on the opposite side of the sight line from the club.

84. What's the occasion?

thrill, excitement

The sign <u>thrill</u> is often used idiomatically to mean, "What's new?" "What's going on?" "Anything exciting happening?" "What's wrong?" "What happened?"

85. We're celebrating our hundreth anniversary.

celebrate   **our**

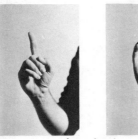

hundred

year

A. In Roman numerals, C=100.

B. There is no sign for "anniversary," substitute <u>year</u>.

86. I didn't know your church was that old. How many years have you been going there?

surprise, awake   how many, how much

A.   In spoken English, the voice emphasizes the word "that" in order to express your surprise. In Ameslan, you sign <u>surprise</u> at the end of the first sentence.

B.   The phrase "been going there," is all implied in two repetitions of the sign <u>go to.</u>

87.   For twenty years.

twenty   up till now

The sign <u>up till now</u> is another time-indicator sign. It means that an action or state of being that began in the past has continued up to the present time, or just recently ended. If there is a number involved in the thought (in this sentence, "twenty") the sign <u>up till now</u> generally preceeds the number.

88.   Do you go to church regularly?

correct, right

When the sign <u>correct</u> is repeated and moved to the side it means "regularly."

89. Every Sunday.

The sign <u>Sunday</u> is moved downwards as you did with "every Saturday," (see 75, A.)

90. Wow! You must be a good boy.

wow

A. Do not sign <u>must</u>, because that sign means "ought to be," "have to be," and that is not the idea expressed in English here.

91. I'm not always good, sometimes I'm bad.

bad

The sign <u>sometimes</u> is two repetitions of the sign <u>once</u> (see 8).

92. I doubt that.

disbelieve, doubt

The sign <u>disbelieve</u> means just that, "not to believe." There is another sign for "doubt" but it means to be unsure of something, not actively to reject it.

93. I'm telling you the truth.

honest

The sign honest is added to the end of the sentence to emphasize your statement, it means "I'm telling you the truth, honest I am."

REVIEW DIALOGUES

94. Try to translate the following dialogues.

translate, interpret

The phrase, "the following dialogues," is signed list converse, or list sentence sentence (see 49,B.).

A.   What do you want to do?
     I don't know, what do you want to do?
     Would you like to watch television?
     It's all right with me.
     What do you want to watch?
     Something funny.
     You like wrestling?
     That's not funny, that's dull.
     There's no football or baseball on.
     Aren't there any good movies on?
     Oh! I forgot I have to go to the club tonight.
     Today's not Saturday.
     That doesn't matter, I've got to rehearse.
     What for? (Just repeat the sign for a couple of times.)
     We're doing a play.

B. I went to my friend's house last night.
What was going on?
He had a captioned film.
Were there many there?
Yes. We ate dinner, and we watched the movie.
Was it a good movie?
It was all right, but there was too much talking, so everyone chatted with each other.
I studied last night.
I don't believe you.
Honest! Ask Joe, he saw me working.
Joe told me he saw you playing cards last night.
That's not so, I haven't played cards in twenty years.

95. Let's sing a song called "Smiles."

Sing, song, music   smile

There is only one sign for "sing," "song," and "music," so sign <u>sing</u> just once.

make, fix   us, we

sad   as, like

51

eyes   fill, full

life   melt, disappear

teardrops   sun

rays   water

wet, damp   warm

love   to, until

There are smiles that make us happy. (A)
There are smiles that make us blue. (B)
There are smiles that steal away the teardrops, (C)
As the sunbeams steal away the dew. (D)
There are smiles that have a tender meaning, (E)
That the eyes of love alone can see. (F)
And the smiles that fill my life with sunshine,
Are the smiles that you gave to me. (G)

A.   For "There are," sign <u>true</u> <u>many</u>.

B.   Since the sign <u>blue</u> refers to the color, sign <u>sad</u>. If a deaf person knows the
      English expression, "I feel blue," then he may sign it <u>blue</u>.

C.   For "steal away," you cannot use the sign <u>steal</u>, since it means "rob."
      Instead, sign <u>melt</u>, which also means disappear.

D.   There is no sign for "dew." Sign <u>water</u> then <u>wet</u>, moving the sign around to
      indicate moisture over a large area.

E.   You could sign <u>soft</u> for "tender," but the author has arbitrarily chosen <u>warm</u>.

F.   For "of," sign <u>fill</u> <u>with</u>. For "alone," sign <u>only</u>. The sentence comes out; <u>that</u>
      <u>eyes</u> <u>fill</u> <u>with</u> <u>love</u> <u>only</u> <u>can</u> <u>see</u>.

G.   For "Are the," sign <u>true</u> <u>like</u>. The expression "you gave to me" would be
      made with just the sign <u>give</u>, moving from the observer towards the signer, in
      ordinary speech. But in poems and songs, we sign <u>you</u> <u>give</u> <u>to</u> <u>me</u> to give it
      more richness, and to keep better time with the music. The sign <u>to</u>, also
      means "until."

LESSON 8
(Dialogue)

96.   Hi! I haven't seen you in a long time.

long   time

The expression, "in a long time" may be translated literally as long time, but it is more idiomatic to use the up till now sign, so the sentence is: see none up till now.

97.   I've been very busy.

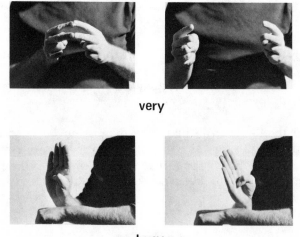

very

busy

The sign busy is an initialized sign (see 19). The letter "B" is attached to the root sign work, and the motion is from side to side. The sign busy also means "business."

98.   What have you been doing?

99. Two weeks ago, I went to the basketball tournament.

week

a week ago

tournament

A. The sign a week ago also means "last week." The alternate way to sign it is week past, but the first way is more idiomatic. To sign "two weeks ago," make the number "2," and execute the same movement as with a week ago. The sign a week ago is a time-indicator sign. When the movement moves forward, rather than backwards over the shoulder, the meaning is "a week from now," "next week," "the coming week," etc., and if the number "2" is used: "two weeks from now," "the next two weeks," etc.

B. By repeating the sign week, you get "weekly," "every week," just as you did with month in 73.

100. Oh! Wonderful, tell me about it!

wonderful

A.   The sign <u>wonderful</u> is almost identical to <u>Sunday</u>. It varies in that it has a slight forward, pushing movement to it.

B.   It is possible to translate "tell me about it" literally, but it is much more idiomatic to sign <u>story</u>. The sign <u>story</u> also means "tell a story," or "relate in story form."

101. It's a long story.

102. I don't care, I've got lots of time.

don't care

There are several ways to sign "don't care," this is just one of them. You may also sign <u>no matter</u> instead of <u>don't care</u>.

103. I left here Friday. The tournament was in Chicago.

here   **depart, leave**

Chicago

There is no need to sign "here," since that is implied in the sign depart.

104. Did you fly or go by train?

airplane, fly

train

which

A.   Again, the signs airplane and train are verbs as well as nouns. The sign airplane means "go by plane." The sign train, however, is often given a slightly different motion when you want to sign "go by train." The noun form has the hand moving back and forth (train); the verb form makes one movement outward ("go by train").

B.   The sign which should come at the end of the statement, since it clearly asks a question regarding a choice between two alternatives. The sentence is signed: airplane train which. There is a sign for "or," but it is not used much, since most questions can be asked better by using the sign which.

105. I flew. It took three hours. When I arrived it was very cold. At first it was raining, then it turned into snow.

hour

require, demand, take

arrive

cold

rain

snow

first

then

all day long

after, across

get out, get off

wait

The sign <u>then</u> literally means "second." The English expression "turn into," when it appears like this, means "become," so sign the meaning (see 58,D.).

It snowed all day long.

The only difference between the signs <u>day</u> and <u>all day long</u> is that the former has only one finger pointing upwards, and the latter has all fingers extended.

After I got off the plane, I waited.

A.   The sign <u>get off</u> also means "to get out of" something. The reverse movement of this sign means "to get into," or "get on" something, usually a vehicle of some sort.

B.   By repeating the sign <u>wait</u> several times, you imply "wait a long time."

106.   Who were you waiting for?

who

Proper English says, "For whom were you waiting?" but Ameslan makes no distinction between "who" and "whom," and you may end a sentence with a preposition.

107. An old friend. We grew up together.

be raised, grow up   while, during

"we went up to him"

become frightened, scare   run away, zoom

sell

___ or (agent sign)

self

A. When the sign grow up uses only one hand, it means a single person. When both hands are used, it means two people grow up together. Thus, it is not necessary to sign with ("together"), however it is often signed for emphasis.

B. Since "we" here means two persons, use the sign we (two persons).

*While I was waiting, I saw a peddler. When my friend arrived, we went up to him.

C. The sign meet is the root sign. Here, one hand is altered so that "two fingers approach one finger," the fingers representing the persons involved. When all five fingers "go up to" one finger, you get "gang up on."

D. Be very much aware of positioning in this sentence. The sign arrive should be on the opposite side of the sight line from the peddler. Then the sign we went up to him should cross the sight line towards the other hand, which is held during this move.

E. The sign ___or is the suffix sign we add to another sign to indicate the person who does the action denoted by the sign. Here it is sell+or which means the person who sells. Airplane+or is "pilot;" run+or is "runner," etc.

We told him to stop, and he got frightened and took off.

F.   When deaf people tell a story involving characters, they assume the roles of the characters and speak their lines. They do not sign, "He said . . . .," they become the character and simply say what the character is supposed to say. So when you sign, "we told him to stop," you should turn facing the peddler, and sign <u>tell stop</u>. When you sign "he got frightened," turn and assume the role of the peddler, and sign <u>frighten</u>. The sign for "run away," which we call the <u>zoom</u> sign, should be made away from where the two friends are standing.

G.   The sign <u>self</u> is more emphatic than merely pointing. You may use it here to indicate the peddler just before turning and signing <u>frighten</u>.

108. Who won the tournament?

win

109. New York won first, and Philadelphia was second.

New York

Philadelphia

first, one dollar

champion

second place

A. Whenever reference is made to positions in any kind of competition, Ameslan signs <u>win</u> <u>first</u>, or <u>champion</u> for "first place." Other places are signed the way "second place" is shown, altering the number, up to five. Beyond five ("fifth place"), we usually switch to the ordinal numbering system.

B. The sign <u>first</u> also means "one dollar," and you must depend upon the context to determine which is meant.

110. Have you traveled much?

It is not necessary to sign, <u>finish</u> <u>travel</u> <u>much</u>, you may condense the sentence to <u>travel</u> <u>much</u>. Naturally, your facial expression will make it clear you are asking a question. Some people conclude that Ameslan is an abbreviated language, a language of short-cuts, and they use such sentences as these for their examples. Ameslan is not an abbreviated language (whatever that might mean), but rather a highly condensed language. This is due to its visual-spatial nature, as opposed to the aural-temporal nature of spoken languages. In the above sentence, there is no abbreviation of meaning, the full meaning is conveyed. However, much of the meaning is communicated non-verbally. The importance of non-verbal cues in Ameslan cannot be overemphasized. We are so conditioned to expressing our ideas in words, that we discount the importance of non-verbal expression.

111. Yes, I've visited many cities.

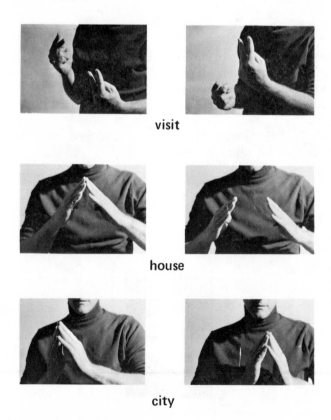

visit

house

city

By repeating the sign <u>house</u>, and moving it in a small circle, we get city.

112. Which cities have you been to?

touch, experience something, been to a place

The sign <u>touch</u> conveys the meaning of the expression "been to" in this sentence.

113. Pittsburgh, New Orleans, San Francisco, Los Angeles, Phoenix, Milwaukee, Washington.

Pittsburgh   New Orleans

San Francisco   Los Angeles

Phoenix   Milwaukee

Washington

114. Have you been to other countries?

country

nation

115. Yes, I've been to Canada, England, France, Germany, and Mexico.

Canada

Germany

France

Mexico

Italy

Holland

Ireland

Scotland

Russia

China

Japan

Spain

England

The sign for "Mexico" varies a great deal. The sign shown here is used in Texas. Ask local deaf people for their sign for Mexico.

116. Is sign language the same all over the world?

same, alike

world

When the sign <u>same</u> is moved around in a horizontal circle, it conveys the idea of "all over," or "all alike."

117. No, it varies, but it's easy to learn new signs.

vary

Do not confuse the sign <u>vary</u> with <u>various</u> (see 65). The sign <u>vary</u> is a verb sign, and <u>various</u> is an adjective sign. It is one of the few signs (like <u>name-christen</u>) that does alter to show a different part of speech.

118. Let's sing another song called "Enjoy Yourself."

This sentence is signed: <u>let sing another</u> <u>name quotations enjoy self</u>. We cannot sign "sing a song" since we <u>have only one</u> sign for both. So, we simply drop one of them.

than   healthy, well, strong

pass, go by   quick, rapid

wink

Enjoy yourself, it's later than you think. (A), (B)
Enjoy yourself, while you're still in the pink.(C)
The years go by as quickly as a wink. (D)
Enjoy yourself, enjoy yourself,
It's later than you think.

A.   When signing poems or songs, we intensify signs, and sign in an elevated heightened manner. Thus <u>enjoy</u> and <u>self</u>, which ordinarily are signed with one hand, are signed with both hands here.

B.   Remember that "it's" is translated to <u>true</u>. In English, the word "later" is used most often in these two situations: (1)when referring to the future: afterwhile, later on, and (2) in making comparisons: "You are later than I am." The first idea is conveyed in Ameslan by the sign <u>afterwhile</u> (see 15), and the second by the signs <u>late</u> and <u>er</u> (see 6,A.). In this song, use the latter signs.

C. The expression "in the pink," like "feeling blue," must not be translated literally unless you are certain your deaf audience knows the expression. Thus, the author has chosen to translate it: <u>feel</u> <u>healthy</u>.

D. The sign <u>year</u> should be repeated to emphasize plurality.

119. Is there any more coffee left?

any

 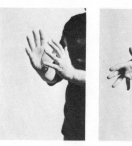

more

coffee

leave, remain

120. There's a little left. Do you like it black?

little, bit

black

All that is needed in the first sentence is the sign <u>little</u>.

121. I use cream and sugar.

cream

sugar

122. I used to drink it that way, but now I take it black.

Translate "used to" as <u>long time ago,</u> when it refers to an habitual action in the past.

123. I've tried to drink it black, but I can't get used to it.

get used to, be used to, habit

Translate "I've tried to drink it black," as <u>try</u> <u>black.</u>

124. The coffee's all gone, you'll have to make some more.

used up, all gone

In sentences 121-124, the English word "use" is shown with four different meanings. Ameslan uses four different signs: (1) "use"—<u>use,</u> (2) "used to"—<u>long time ago,</u> (3) "get used to"—<u>habit,</u> (4) "used up"—<u>used up.</u> You must first determine exactly what a word means, then sign the meaning. Words stand for meanings; signs stand for meanings; signs do not stand for words.

125. I always get stuck with the empty pot.

get stuck, hung up   **empty, vacant, blank, naked**

There is no sign for "pot." You must use a mime that resembles the shape of the pot, or else you simply omit "empty pot," and sign I always stuck. Here you would sign "I" to emphasize the point. Another very idiomatic way to convey the idea that the same old thing keeps happening is to sign same (see 116) with one hand, and move it in a vertical circle several times.

126. I hate making coffee, I don't know how.

hate

127. It's useless for me to make coffee.

worth, value, important

useless, no value, worthless

128. Me too.

Use the sign <u>same</u> (see 116), but move it back and forth between you and the other person.

129. My coffee tastes terrible. Why are you laughing?

taste

laugh

The second sentence may be signed just <u>laugh</u>, followed by a shrug with palms up and outstretched towards the observer. This is an emphatic way to ask a question.

130. I can't help it! You look so funny.

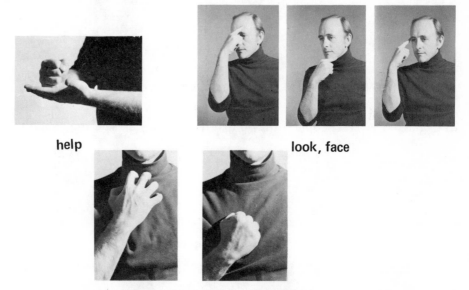

help

look, face

stifle a laugh or an emotion, restrain

A.   Instead of signing, <u>can't help</u>, sign <u>can't stifle</u>.

B.   Be careful when translating the English word, "look." If it means "look at," sign <u>watch</u> (see 59). If it means "look like," sign <u>face.</u>

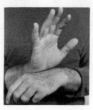

131. Yesterday, I found five dollars at work.

yesterday   **find**

fifth, five dollars

There is no sign for "at," so point to where your work is.

132. I asked several people if they'd lost it, and they all said they hadn't.

ask a question

several, few

lose

A.   The sign ask question is extremely versatile. When you sign it towards the observer, it means, "I ask you." When the signer signs it towards himself, coming from the observer, it means "You ask me." When the signer signs it towards himeself coming from an angle to the sight line, it means "(a third person or persons) ask me." To convey the idea, "I asked several people," move the sign in an arc as you repeat it, as if the people you asked were standing there in front of you. When the sign is done with both hands along the sight line, it means, "test," "examination," "quiz," "interrogation," etc. When the sign is made with both hands, moved downwards while being repeated, it means "questionnaire," "survey form," etc. Finally, there is an idiomatic use of the sign. When in English, we respond to a question with a statement such as, "I think so, don't you?" or "Do you really think so?" the sign ask question is used for the "don't you" in the first example, and for the whole sentence in the second example. The sign ask question is reviewed in Appendix B.

B.   For the clause, "if they'd lost it," simply sign lose. Since it follows the sign ask question, the meaning is quite clear. Ameslan generally avoids the English "if" whenever possible. Some examples of this are:

I asked you if you wanted to go (ask question want go).
You told me you'd stay if I would (you tell me you stay I stay with).
If you do that, I won't go (you perform that I refuse go).

C.   For the clause, "they all said they hadn't," just sign none. The implication is that "no one responded to the question."

133.   One girl asked me where I found it.

girl

Remember the "asked me" translated by the sign ask question, made towards the signer from an angle to the sight line.

134.   She told me she had lost five dollars.

The first "she" is indicated by pointing, which is blended into the "tell me," then the second "she" is signed self.

135. I told her I didn't think it was hers.

The possessive pronouns are all signed alike, varying only in the direction of the sign: <u>my</u>, <u>mine</u> (towards the signer), <u>your</u>, <u>yours</u> (towards the observer/s), <u>their</u>, <u>theirs</u>, <u>his</u>, <u>her</u>, <u>hers</u> (towards the area where the third person/s are located).

136. She asked me how I knew.

137. I told her I found it in the men's room.

toilet

"Men's room," is signed <u>man</u> <u>toilet</u>.

138. She was really embarrassed!

red   **embarrass**

Sometimes the sign <u>red</u> preceeds <u>embarrassed</u>, sometimes it is not used at all. There are several ways to sign "embarrassment." Since they are highly local signs, you should ask a deaf person, or your teacher to show you the local sign.

139. Did you clean your room?

clean, nice

room

When <u>clean</u> is done with one movement, it means "nice," "clean" (adj.). When the movement is repeated, it means "clean up" (v.).

140. Not yet.

141. Why haven't you?

142. I got up late.

get up

A.   Here the <u>late</u> sign means "tardy." The context tells whether the sign means "tardy" or whether it means that something has not yet happened.

B.   The sign <u>get up</u> means to arise from a prone position ("Get out of bed." "Get up off the floor."), or to stand up ("Get up out of your chairs.")'

143. You over sleep all the time.

over sleep, sun up

The sign <u>sun up</u> may mean "sunrise" or "oversleep." When it is repeated two or three times it means that a person habitually oversleeps. The opposite movement of this sign means "sunset."

144. Stop picking on me.

pick on someone

A.   Be sure to make the sign <u>pick on</u> towards yourself to imply "me."

B.   This sentence should be signed: <u>pick on me</u> <u>finish.</u> It illustrates an idiomatic use of the sign <u>finish</u>. Often, if one person is angry at another for persisting in doing something annoying, he will sign to the person, <u>finish</u>. It means, "If you do that again, I'm liable to bust you in the mouth!"

145. Have you swept and washed the dishes yet?

sweep   **wash dishes**

The sign <u>wash</u> will vary depending upon what you are washing.

146. I will afterwhile.

will, shall, future

The sign <u>will</u> is a time indicator sign.

147. You're always saying you'll do it later, but you never do.

say, speak

postpone, put off

never

This sentence is signed: <u>always</u> <u>say</u> <u>afterwhile</u> <u>afterwhile</u> <u>postpone</u> <u>postpone</u> <u>postpone</u> <u>never</u>. The repetitions of <u>afterwhile</u> and <u>postpone</u> emphasize the habitual action. The repetitions of <u>postpone</u> should move farther and farther into the future, i.e., away from the signer.

148. That's a lie!

lie, falsehood

149. Call me a liar and I won't help you.

refuse, won't

> Translate "Call me" with the <u>name</u> sign moving towards you along the sight line, while the sign <u>help</u> should move toward the observer to imply "help you."

150. Will you please stop!

151. All right, do as you please.

do as one wishes

> Literally, the sign means "think for yourself."

152. From now on, mind your own business.

after, from now on   **pay attention, attend to, mind, concentrate**

153. Wait 'till Mom sees your room. She said you couldn't go out to play until your room was cleaned.

mother

forbid, prohibit, illegal

out

A.   The pronoun "She" in the second sentence, should be signed <u>mother</u>. Repeat the sign for the antecedent if pointing, or the sign <u>self</u> might not make it clear.

B.   The <u>can't</u> sign is also used for "couldn't," but in this case the <u>illegal</u> sign is much stronger. Use the <u>can't</u> sign in such sentences as, "I couldn't see." Use the <u>illegal</u> sign to indicate that something is against the rules, or is illegal, or carries punishment.

154. I'll clean it before Mom gets home.

before

A. "I'll" is translated simply as <u>will</u>.

B. "Gets home" is signed <u>arrive</u>, while "home" is dropped since it is understood.

155. She's gonna be mad at you.

cross, angry

156. Well, I'm mad at you.

angry, furious

157. Where are your dirty clothes?

dirty

clothes, wear, dress, get dressed

158. I put them in the washing machine.

put, place, move   **washing machine**

The sign <u>washing machine</u> is also used for "laundramat." The sign <u>put</u> will vary considerably according to what you put where. You should mime it, making the same motion you actually do when you put clothes in a machine.

159. Why didn't you wait?

160. Wait for what?

By repeating the sign <u>for</u> you get "What for?" "What's that for?" (see Review Dialogue 94,A.)

161. I wanted to put mine in with them.

The sign <u>with</u> implies "in with them" when you make the movement towards the washing machine (see 82,B.)

162. Sorry, you're too slow.

slow

Make the sign <u>slow</u> very slowly to emphasize the point.

163. You're so stubborn.

stubborn

164. So are you!

The sign <u>same</u> is done with one hand quickly and with vigor.

165. You won't get to go to the movies.

166. And I won't tell you a secret.

secret

Notice that "won't" in the previous sentence is signed <u>not</u>, and in this sentence is signed <u>refuse.</u> The first is a simple statement of fact, the second is a statement of determination not to do something. Decide which way "won't" should be signed in these sentences:

The shoe won't fit.
The car won't go.
Why won't you tell me?
He won't play.

Be careful with the last sentence. If the context were about an athlete, and you were discussing whether he will play, you must know why he "won't" play. Is his leg broken? If so, you sign can't. If he's angry at the coach, sign refuse.

167. What secret.

168. The washing machine's broken.

break

169. Stupid!

stupid, dumb

170. Moron!

extremely dumb

We call this sign tiny blockhead.

171. Another song called "Linger Awhile."

star

shone, glow, glitter

above, overhead

stay, remain, linger

they (stars)

whisper

seem, appear

The stars shine above you, yet linger awhile. (A), (B), (C)
They whisper, I love you, so linger awhile. (D), (E)
And when you have gone away,
Each hour will seem a day. (F)
I've something to tell you, so linger awhile.

A. The sign shine actually comes off the back of the hand. But, when you refer to an object shining ("stars" in this case), use both hands and associate them with the object.

B. The sign above is usually done at chest level. Here it is done above the head to continue with the visualization of the stars overhead.

C. Here the word "yet" means "but," so sign but.

86

D. The sign <u>talk</u> is done with two hands, with the fingers gently moving. Bend over slightly. This conveys the idea of "whisper."

E. Translate "so" to <u>please</u>.

F. The sign <u>seem</u> is usually followed by the sign <u>as</u> (like, same).

172. What happened to you! How did you get that black eye? Did somebody hit you?

happen   **black eye**

strike, or hit someone

A.   This sentence may be signed in a variety of ways. Here are some options:

how happen black (circle around the eye).
how happen black eye
thrill black eye (see 84)

B.   "Someone" and "something" are usually conveyed with the same sign, the only sign. However, "someone" may be signed only person, and "something" as only thing.

173. Yes, but it wasn't a fight.

fight

174. Last night, I was sitting, reading a book.

sit

A. The sign yesterday is a time indicator sign. It is often combined with the sign night to make "last night." Equally as common is to sign "last night" as past night.

B. The sign read should follow book, and should be repeated several times. By doing this, you create a natural and interesting bridge to the next idea. The "vibration" will interrupt the "reading."

175. I felt a vibration.

vibration, shaking

The sign vibration is varied to indicate the kind and intensity of the vibration. Here the kind is a mild, back and forth one.

*176. My light was broken, so I went to the door, because I thought someone might be knocking, but there was no one there.

electric light

"go to the door"

door   **"knocking on the door"**

A. The sign <u>electric</u> <u>light</u> is highly local, so check with deaf people in your area for their sign.

B. The sign <u>door</u> may also mean "open the door." To "close the door," reverse the movement.

C. Here again, your index finger becomes the storyteller, and "goes to the door," (see 107,C.).

D. Mime "knocking on the door."

E. The signing order must be changed from English word order, so as to create a clearer visualization. Here is one option:

<u>my</u> <u>light</u> <u>break</u> <u>think</u> <u>maybe</u> <u>someone</u> (knock on the door) <u>get</u> <u>up</u> (index finger goes to the door) <u>open</u> <u>door</u> <u>none</u>.

177. I figured it was probably an airplane.

A. For "figured," sign <u>seem</u>, which implies "probably" so there is no need to sign <u>maybe</u>.

B. The <u>seem</u> <u>airplane</u> signs should be done as if the signer were talking to himself as he did when it really happened the night before. As a matter of fact, except when the signer is addressing the observer directly, the whole story should be delivered as a re-enactment.

C. The Ameslan would add at the end of this sentence the sign <u>close door</u>.

178. I sat down and started reading again.

begin, start

Again, make the sign <u>read</u> last in the sentence to provide the bridge to the next thought.

179. The vibration came again.

The word "came" is not translated.

180. I began to get a little bit frightened.

The sign <u>fright</u> should be less intense than it was in 107.

181. I wondered what was happening.

The sign <u>wonder</u> is similar to <u>think</u> (46,A.), except that it is larger in size.

182. I tiptoed to the window and looked out all over the place, but I didn't see a thing.

tiptoe   **window**

    A.   The index fingers here become your legs. Move them gingerly as if they were tiptoeing.

    B.   The sign <u>look at</u> should be used, and it should actually "look out all over."

    C.   The clause "but I didn't see a thing," is signed simply <u>none</u>.

183. Then I remembered that my father was upstairs.

father

    A.   When you sign <u>remember,</u> your face must show that you "just remembered!"

    B.   To indicate "upstairs" and "downstairs," merely point in the appropriate direction.

184. I thought he might be sick and was banging on the floor.

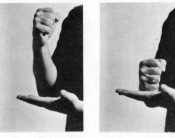

"pound on the floor"   **floor**

The sign used here for "floor" can be any flat surface, therefore, it should be made down towards the floor, or should be reinforced by point to the floor.

185. I dashed up the stairs.

"Quick up the stairs."

All you need to sign here is <u>run</u> (see 65), or <u>quick</u>, but the movement must be made upwards, toward "upstairs."

186. I flung open the door and there was my father jumping up and down doing calesthentics.

stand   **jump up and down**

exercise

For "doing calesthentics" sign <u>exercise</u>.

187. I went in and tapped him on the shoulder, but his fist accidentally hit me in the eye.

enter

accident, mistake, wrong   **"hit in the eye"**

A.   For "tap him on the shoulder," mime the action.

B.   The sign <u>mistake</u> must follow the "tapping on the shoulder." It sets the scene, and cues the observer that what happens next was an accident, was a mistake, was not intended.

C.   For "his fist accidentally hit me in the eye," mime the action.

NOTES

72. Deaf people are restricted in the number of films they can enjoy. Dialogue and off-camera narration play an important role in most movies, thus deaf people find it difficult to follow the story of the film. They do enjoy foreign films with sub-titles, and films where the action and not the dialogue carries the story. To provide more films for deaf people, the United States Congress established an agency within the Department of Health, Education, and Welfare to purchase or lease films, put sub-titles on them, and distribute them free of charge to deaf groups. This program is referred to as Captioned Films for the Deaf.

75. Nearly every city in the United States with a sizable population of deaf people, will have a club. The club may be as small as a monthly get together in a rented park, or recreation center, or as large as a multistoried building open every weekend, and sometimes during the week. The club is the social center for most deaf people. They go there to see each other, socialize, and talk. Many clubs sponsor bowling, softball, and basketball teams that compete in leagues for hearing people. Once a year, there is a national basketball tournament, where the clubs compete for the national championship. The tournament is sponsored by the American Athletic Association of the Deaf, which is made up of the clubs. Once every four years, the A.A.A.D. sponsors a team to compete in the International Games for the Deaf, the "Deaf Olympics."

107. The sign sell—seller has a very specific meaning among deaf people. It refers to those few deaf people who sell alphabet cards and other trinkets. Deaf people generally dislike these peddlers, and discourage hearing people from buying from them, since it perpetrates the image among the public that deaf people are unable to keep gainfully employed. A few states have outlawed these peddlers. Peddling is a nationally syndicated racket, so to patronize it is to support an organized racket that exploits deafness. If you are a salesman, it is best if you sign, "I work in a store", (the sign for store varies locally, but you may sign sell for "store"), or "I sell cars", "I sell houses", etc.

176. Deaf people are super-sensitive to tactile vibrations. Any loud bang or knock will often get their attention, since they can feel the noise. Many deaf people have installed in their homes electric lights, hooked up to the door bell. When the button is pressed, the light flashes. If they have no such light, you must bang on the door in hopes they will feel it.

APPENDIX A

Time Indicator Signs

These are the signs used to establish when an event or action occurs. The past-time indicators (except for the up till now sign) always move backwards, i.e. toward the area behind the signer. Future-time indicators move forward. The present-time indicator moves downward.

Future Time
  1. later, afterwhile

      This sign is altered to give "in a moment," and "much later on."
  2. tomorrow
 *3. day after tomorrow, two days from now
**4. next week, two weeks from now
  5. next
  6. next year, two years from now
  7. will, shall, future
  9. a long time into the future

Present Time

  1. now, to (___day, ___night)
  2. this (_____afternoon, _____morning)

Past Time

  1. recent, a moment ago
  2. awhile ago
  3. yesterday
 *4. day before yesterday, two days ago
**5. last week, two weeks ago
  6. past, last (___night, ___week, ___month)
**7. a year ago, last year, two years ago
  8. a long time ago
***9. up till now

Special Time Indicators

The signs finish and not yet (late) refer specifically to whether an action has, or has not been completed.

   *   These signs are highly local. Check with local deaf people. Fortunately, they are rarely used.
  **   There are two ways to sign "next week," and "next year:" (1) make the two signs next week, and next year, and (2) make the single sign for them. The same holds for "last week," and "last year" (1) sign past week and past year, or (2) last week and last year. In both these cases, the second way is the more idiomatic.
***   The sign up till now moves from the back towards the front, since it indicates an action that began in the past and has continued to the present, or just recently ended.

95

The Sign ask question

This sign is altered in meaning when its direction of movement is altered, and when it uses one or two hands.

I.   One Hand
    A.   Simple Asking
        1. I ask you.
        2. You ask me.
        3. He asks me.
        4. I ask him.

    B.   Complex Asking
        1. I ask a lot of people.
        2. You keep asking me.

    C.   Idiomatic Use
        1. Do you think so?
        2. Do you?
        3. To emphasize a question.

II. Two Hands
    A.   examination, quiz
    B.   survey form, questionnaire
    C.   interrogation, interview
        1. of others—movement away from the signer
        2. of oneself—movement toward the signer
    E.   ask each other, correspond (there is another sign for "correspond" besides this one)

BIBLIOGRAPHY

All of the following books may be purchased from the National Association of the Deaf, 814 Thayer Avenue, Silver Spring, Maryland, 20910.

AMESLAN TEXTS

Falberg, Roger M., The Language of Silence
Fant, Louie J., Jr., Ameslan, An Introduction to American Sign Language
Madsen, Willard, Conversational Sign Language: An Intermediate Manual

SIGLISH AND OTHER TEXTS

Babbini, Barbara, Manual Communication, Fingerspelling and the Language of Signs: A Course of Study Outline for Students.
Fant, Louie, Jr., Say It With Hands
Guillory, LaVera M., Expressive and Receptive Fingerspelling for Hearing Adults
Gustason, Gerilee, et.a., Signing Exact English
O'Rourke, Terrence, A Basic Course in Manual Communication

DICTIONARIES

Benson, Elizabeth, Sign Language
Davis, Anne, The Language of Signs
Kannapell, Barbara M., et al, Signs: For Instructional Purposes
Riekehof, Lottie, Talk to the Deaf
Springer, C.F., Talking With the Deaf
Stokoe, William C., et al, Dictionary of American Sign Language
Watson, David O., Talk With Your Hands

about—51
above—171
absurd—81
accident—187
across—105
act (drama)—60
action—62
actual—2
actually—2
after—105, 152
afternoon—1
afterwhile—15
again—38
ago—52
airplane—104
alike—116
all—53
all day—105
all gone—124
all kinds of—65
all right—12
allow—38
almost—53
alone—50
always—50
Ameslan—27
and—41
angry—155, 156
another—66
any—119
anyhow—79
appear—171
arrive—105
as—95
ask—47
ask a question—132, A.
associate—77
attempt—34
attend to—152
attention—152
awake—86
awful—5
awhile—15
awhile ago—30

bad—91
banquet—83
baseball—65
basketball—65
because—22
become—58

before—154
begin—178
best—6
better—6
birth—58
black—120
black eye—172
blank—125
book—27
boring—63
born—58
borrow—52
boy—67
break—168
bury—58
busy—97
but—31

call—27
can—80
Canada—115
can't—80
captioned—19 (see 69,A.)
card playing—77
celebrate—85
certain—2
certainly—2
champion—109
chat—77, C.
Chicago—103
China—115
christen—27
church—83
city—111
class—17
clean—139
clear—70
clothes—157
club—75
coffee—119
cold—105
compete—65
complete—28
comprehend—12
concentrate—152
confuse—35
converse—22
could—80
couldn't—80
country—114
correct—88

cow—67
cream—121
create—56
cross (angry)—155

damp—95
day—1
deaf—22
decline (in health)—58, D.
deamnd—105
depart—103
desire—31
die—58
different—31
difficult—24
dirty—157
disappear—95
disbelieve—92
do—16
do as one wishes—151
doesn't matter—79
dominoes—77
don't—13
don't care—102
don't know—78
don't want—78
door—176
doubt—92
dull (boring)—63
dumb—169
drama—60
dress—157
dry—63
during—107

each—70
each other—77
easy—23
eat—28
electric light—176
else—66
embarrass—138
empty—125
England—115
enjoy—13
enough—36
enter—187
___er—6
etcetera—65
every—70

98

every (∴ day of the
    week)—75, A.
excitement—84
excellent—5
excuse—11
exercise—186
experience something—112
extremely dumb—170
eyes—95

face—130
father—183
fatigued—5
feel—4
fellowship—77
few—132
fifth—131
fight—173
fill—95
find—131
fine—5
finish—28
first—105, 109
five dollars—131
fix—95
floor—184
fly (plane)—104
food—28
foolish—81
football—65
for—49
forbid—153
forgive—11
forget—50
France—115
Friday—58
friend—44
fright—107
from—72
from now on—152
funny—68
furious—156
future—146
full—95

Germany—115
get—72
get in—105
get off—105
get out—105
get stuck—125

get up—142, B.
get used to—123
girl—133
give—44
glad—2
glitter—171
glow—171
go—14
go to—74
go away—48
go by—118
good—1
goodbye—15
good morning—1
good night—1
got to—14
government—72
grave—58
group—17
grow up—107, A.

habit—123
happen—172
happy—2
hard—24
hate—126
have—53
have to—14
healthy—118
hello—2
help—130
here—103
hit—172
Holland—115
home—74
honest—93
hour—105
house—111
how—3
how many—86
how much—86
hundred—85
hung up—125
hungry—31
hunt—67

I—2
ill—5
illegal—153
important—127
in—17

indeed—2
intend—33
intention—33
interact—77
interested—59
interpret—94
invent—56
Ireland—115
irrespective—79
Italy—115

Japan—115
jump up and down—186

know—78

language—19
last (night)—52, A.
last week—98
late—29
later—15
laugh—129
learn—18
leave (depart)—103
leave (remain)—119
lend—52
let—38
lie (false)—148
life—95
light—176
like—59
like (as)—95
linger—171
list—49
little—120
long—96
long time ago—69
look (like)—130
look at—59
Los Angeles—113
lose—132
lots of—61, A.
lousy—5
love—95

make—95
man—67, B.
many—25
marry—58
maybe—36
meaning—33

me—2
meet—7
meet you—7
meet many people—77, A.
melt—95
memorize—49
men—67, B.
mention—27
Mexico—115
Milwaukee—113
mind one's business—152
mistake—187
mix—35
Monday—58
month—73
monthly—73
more—119
morning—1
most—39
mother—153
move—158
movie—48
much—61, A.
music—95
must—14
my—42

naked—125
name—27, 53
nation—114,
necessary—14
need—14
need to—14
never—147
nevertheless—79
new—23
New Orleans—113
New York—109
newspaper—43
next—82
nice—139
night—1
no—10
no one—55, B.
no value—127
none—55, B.
not—8
not yet—29
nothing—55, B.
now—14

often—34
okay—82
old—69
on—32
once—8
one dollar—109, B.
only—50
__or—107, E.
other—66
ought—14
our—85
out—153
oversleep—143

page of—49
paper—43
pardon—11
pass—118
past—52
pay attention to—152
people—22
perform—16
perhaps—36
permit—38
Philadelphia—109
Phoenix—113
pick on—144
Pittsburgh—113
place—158
play (games)—77
play (drama)—60
play (cards)—77
please—13
plenty—36
poem—58
poetry—58
possess—53
postpone—147
practice—31
print—43
prohibit—153
purpose—33
put—158
put off—147

quick—118
quotation marks—58
quiet—69

rain—105
rapid—118
raised (grow up)—107, A.
rays (sun)—95
read—45
real—2
really—2
recall—8
receive—72
red—138
refuse—149
regardless—79
regret—11
regularly—88
remain (left)—119
remain (stay)—171
remember—8
restrain (an impulse)—130
request—47
require—105
rediculous—81
right (correct)—88
room—139
run—65
run away quickly—107
Russia—115

sad—95
same—116
San Francisco—113
say—147
Saturday—58
scare—107
Scotland—115
second place—109, A.
see—2
seems—171
secret—166
self—107, G.
sell—107
sentence—19
several—132
shall—146
shine—171
should—14
show (drama)—60
sick—5
sign—17
silent—69
silly—81
simple—23

sing—95
sit—174
slow—162
smile—95
snow—105
Solomon Grundy—58, B.
some—33
someone—50
something—50
sometimes—91
song—95
sorry—11
Spain—115
speak—147
stand—186
star—171
start—178
stay—171
stifle—130
still—32
stop—81
story—58
strike—172
strong—118
stubborn—163
study—24
stupid—169
sugar—121
sun—95
Sunday—58
sunrise—143
sunset—143
superb—5
supposed to—14
sure—2
surely—2
surprise—86
sweep—145
swim—65

take up—17
takes (requires)—105
talk—61, B.
talk to—22
tardy—29
taste—129
teardrops—95
television—59
tell—50
terrible—5
than—118

thank you—5
that—37
then—105
thing—49
think—46
this (morning)—71
thrill—84
Thursday—58
time—96
tiptoe—182
tired—5
to—95
today—71
together—22
toilet—137
tonight—71
touch—112
tournament—99
train—104
training—31
translate—94
travel—67
trouble—40
truly—2
true—2
truth—2
try—34
Tuesday—58
twenty—87
typewriter—42

understand—12
until—95
up till now—87
us (two persons)—8
us (more than
    two persons)—95
use—34
used to—122
used to (get used to,
            be used to)—123
used up—124
useless—127

vacant—125
value—127
various—65
vary—117
very—97
vibration—175
visit—111

wait—105
want—22
war—67
warm—95
washing machine—158
Washington—113
wash dishes—145
watch—59
water—95
we (two persons)—8
we (more than two persons)—95
wear (clothes)—157
weary—5
Wednesday—58
week—99
week ago—99, A.
well—118
wet—95
what—16
when—70
where—42
while—107
which—104
whisper—171
who—106
why—21
will—146
win—108
wink—118
window—182
wish—31
with—22
wonder—181
wonderful—100
won't—149
work—32
world—116
worn out—5
worry—40
worth—127
worthless—127
Wow!—90
wrestle—65
wrong—187
year—85
yes—9
yesterday—131
yet (but)—31
yet (still)—32
you—2
your—44
zoom—107, F.